SPOTTER'S GUIDE TO
CATS

Howard Loxton

Illustrated by David Astin, Denise ~~Finney~~,
David Hurrell and David Wright

Edited by Laura Howell, Bridget Gibbs
and Felicity Mansfield
Designed by Candice Whatmore
Series designer: Laura Fearn
Consultant: Amanda Thomas

Picture acknowledgements: Cover © Jane Burton;
pages 4-5, 10, 13 © Jane Burton; backgrounds - pages 24-25,
60-62 © Digital Vision.

First published in 2001 by Usborne Publishing Ltd.,
Usborne House, 83-85 Saffron Hill, London, EC1N 8RT, England.
www.usborne.com

Printed in Spain

CONTENTS

HOW TO USE THIS BOOK

This book is a guide to identifying different cat breeds. The cats in the book are arranged by colour to make it easier for you to look them up. Pages 48 to 54 also show some examples of common cat behaviour.

When you have seen a particular type of cat or behaviour, you can tick it off in the circle next to the appropriate picture.

Most of the illustrations in this book are of pure-bred cats. These are cats whose ancestors (parents, grandparents and so on) were all the same breed.

Some pure-bred cats, such as the Manx or Sphynx, are instantly recognizable. Others look very similar to mixed-breeds. For example, you may spot a tabby cat which looks very similar to a pure-bred tabby. You can tick off any cat you see that looks like one in this book.

A cat's height is measured from its front paws to its shoulders. Most domestic cats are of a similar size.

Height

IDENTIFYING FEATURES

The description next to each cat will help you to identify it. In some cases, this includes parts of the "breed standard". This is a set of ideal features which official cat associations decide each breed should have. The eye colour given in each description is usually that of the breed standard. Most cats are not pure-bred, and do not have every feature.

This is a mixed-breed kitten. Each of its parents was a cross between two different pure breeds.

CHECKLIST

At the end of the book, you will find a checklist of all the cat breeds and behaviours described on pages 14 to 54. When you have spotted a breed or behaviour, use the checklist to record the date on which you saw it.

Name of breed	Date spotted
Colourpoint, Tortie	10/1
Cream Longhair	8/6
Cream Shorthair	12/2
Cymric	9/9

Fill in the checklist like this.

BODY TYPES

Cats are divided into three main groups according to their build or shape. The groups are: Shorthair (British, European and American), Longhair, and Foreign. In each group there are many coat colours and patterns.

SHORTHAIRS

The ideal Shorthair has a sturdy, powerful body and short, strong legs with rounded paws. Its head is broad and round with a short, straight nose, full cheeks and big eyes. Its ears are small and set wide apart.

Shorthairs' tails are thick at the base and taper slightly. Their fur is short and dense. The cat on the right is a British Shorthair, but European and American Shorthairs are very similar.

British Shorthair

Thick tail with rounded tip

Rounded ears

Short, dense fur

Round eyes

Full cheeks

Strong, short legs

Neat, round paws

This American Wirehair is an example of an American Shorthair type cat. Its body is a little less "cobby" (broad and sturdy) than a British Shorthair's.

This breed has unusual wiry fur

LONGHAIRS

The most important feature of a Longhair (also called a Persian) is its long, silky fur. Extra-long fur forms a ruff around its face and continues in a frill between its front legs. A Longhair has a large, stocky body and short, thick legs with round, firm paws. Its round head has full cheeks, a snub nose and large eyes. Its ears are small, with long tufts of fur growing inside them. The tail is short and bushy.

Small ears, set wide apart

Bushy tail

Ear tufts

Long coat

Ruff

Fur "breeches" on back legs

Frill

Short, thick legs

Round, firm paws

FOREIGN CATS

A Foreign cat has a long body with slender legs and a long, tapering tail. Its wedge-shaped head has large, pricked ears and slanting, almond-shaped eyes. Its fur is short and sleek. Most non-British, American or European shorthaired cats are of this type. Some Foreign cats are also known as Orientals.

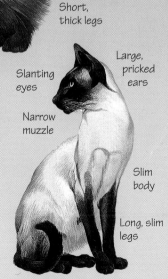

Large, pricked ears

Slanting eyes

Narrow muzzle

Slim body

Long, slim legs

Neat, oval paws

COAT PATTERNS

A cat's fur, called its coat, is made up of two layers - soft, warm underfur and a rough, protective top coat. The coat, which can be many different shades, may be "self-coloured" (plain) or marked with patches. Patterns of stripes or spots are called "tabby markings", and are very common. The three basic types are described here.

CLASSIC TABBY

Classic Tabby markings are the most common. The pattern includes rings around the legs and tail, stripes across the chest called "mayoral chains", fine lines on the side of the face called "pencilling" and an M-shaped mark on the forehead. There is also a round mark on the cat's side called the "poached-egg-on-toast" mark, and a butterfly-shaped mark on the shoulders.

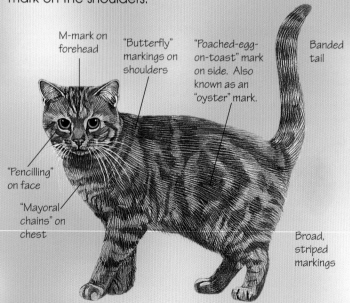

M-mark on forehead

"Butterfly" markings on shoulders

"Poached-egg-on-toast" mark on side. Also known as an "oyster" mark.

Banded tail

"Pencilling" on face

"Mayoral chains" on chest

Broad, striped markings

MACKEREL TABBY

Mackerel Tabby markings are less common: they are hardly ever seen on Longhairs. In this pattern, the Classic Tabby's body markings are replaced by narrow vertical stripes running from the spine down to the belly.

Narrow,
vertical
stripes

SPOTTED SHORTHAIR

Spotted Shorthair markings developed from Mackerel Tabby markings. In this coat pattern, the Mackerel Tabby's stripes are broken up into clearly defined spots.

Spotted
coat

Broken
stripes
on tail

BODY FEATURES

In addition to all-over patterns and markings, many cats have individual body features which help you to identify them. Here are some of the features to look out for.

A **blaze** is a wide flash of a contrasting colour down the centre of a cat's face. Blazes are often light-coloured.

Red blaze   White blaze

This cat has brick red nose leather

Whiskers

Blackish paw pads

Nose leather is the skin at the end of a cat's nose.

Whiskers are long, sensitive bristles on cats' faces which help them feel their way around, especially at night. A cat's whiskers match or tone with its coat colour.

Paw pads are the cushion-like pads of skin under a cat's paws. Nose leather and paw pads are usually the same colour. They match or tone with the cat's coat.

TIPPING

Some cats have tipped fur. This means that the tip contrasts with the colour of the rest of the hair. British Tipped Shorthairs, for example, have white fur tipped with black. A tipped coat appears to sparkle as the cat moves.

White hair

Black tip

TICKING

Ticked fur produces a coat that looks speckled, and is only seen on Abyssinian cats. The main colour of each hair is broken up by two or three bands of a contrasting colour.

Red hair

Black bands

POINTS

A cat's legs, paws, tail, ears, and mask (face) are known as its "points". Some cats, such as Siamese cats, have pale coats with points of a contrasting colour.

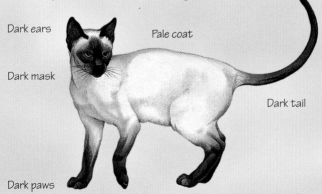

Dark ears

Pale coat

Dark mask

Dark tail

Dark paws

BREEDING

Like all animals, cats inherit their shape, colour and other characteristics from their parents. Most features can be predicted if the family trees of both parents are known.

Some characteristics are dominant, that is, their presence masks other characteristics.

Tortoiseshell and White kitten

If parents each have different characteristics, most of their kittens will show the dominant ones. Tabby markings, for instance, are a dominant characteristic. This is why there are so many tabbies and cats with tabby markings. Certain characteristics are only carried by one sex. For instance, red or cream cats are nearly always male.

PEDIGREE CATS

A pedigree cat has a recorded family tree which traces the breeds of its ancestors for at least three generations.

Tortoiseshell colouring is inherited from red or tortoiseshell parents. Kittens of this kind are almost always female.

SHOWING CATS

There are many organizations around the world which deal with breeding and showing pedigree cats. In some countries, such as the USA, there are a number of independent governing bodies. In Britain, the Governing Council of the Cat Fancy (GCCF) links all the local organizations and groups associated with particular breeds.

The GCCF controls the recognition of new cat breeds, keeps a register of pedigree cats, organizes shows and decides breed standards. The Fédération Internationale Féline (FIFe) is the GCCF's European equivalent, and there are many others around the world. You can find out how to contact all of these organizations on page 59.

GOING TO CAT SHOWS

You can look in local newspapers and cat magazines for details of cat shows organized by the local governing body or by cat clubs.

Many of the Web sites listed on page 59 have details of larger shows organized by cat clubs around the world.

Here are some features that this breed (a Blue Tortoiseshell Birman) should have to be entered in a show.

Ears set well apart

Broad, rounded head

Round, deep blue eyes

Full, round cheeks

Full ruff around neck

Long, silky coat

Bushy, medium length tail (not visible here)

Thick legs

RED CATS

Red cats have rich, orangey-red fur. Some red cats are ginger or sandy-coloured, but the breed standard requires a deep orangey or coppery tinge to the coat.

Ears are tufted

◀ RED OR SORREL ABYSSINIAN

A Foreign cat with a ticked top coat. Each hair is a coppery red, with bands of chocolate brown. Its underfur is apricot. Green, gold or hazel eyes, outlined in black.

Tail has a solid chocolate-brown tip

➡ RED SELF LONGHAIR

This longhaired cat's coat should be an even colour all over, but may still have tabby markings. Its body is low and sturdy, and its legs are short. Orange or copper eyes.

Long, silky ruff

Short, bushy tail

◀ RED BURMESE

This heavily-built cat of Foreign type has a light, tangerine coat, sometimes with faint tabby markings. Golden yellow eyes.

BLACK CATS

Although black cats with white markings are very common, show-standard cats must not have any white hair in their coats. The colour of a pure black coat can be affected by exposure to strong light.

➡ BLACK SHORTHAIR
This cat has the powerful, compact body of a British Shorthair. Sunbathing may give its black coat a rusty tinge. Orange or copper eyes.

Coat should be pure black

⬅ FOREIGN BLACK
Developed from Siamese cats, this elegant cat has a Foreign type body and a narrow, wedge-shaped head. The ideal coat is pure, jet black. Green, slanting eyes.

➡ BLACK LONGHAIR
This cat has a long, pure black coat, which may turn rusty through too much sunbathing or washing. Copper or deep orange eyes.

Black Longhair kittens often have a rusty tinge

BLUE CATS

Blue cats have blue-grey fur. Blue is a dilute form of black in cats. Blue cats often have gentle natures.

◄ BRITISH BLUE
A good example of a British Shorthair. This cat has a low, stocky body and a broad, round head with big cheeks. Its blue coat is lightly ticked on the shoulders. Rich orange, yellow or copper eyes.

Feet have silvery sheen

➡ RUSSIAN BLUE
A small, dainty cat of Foreign type. Its ears are large and paper-thin. Its silvery blue coat is short and thick. Quiet and sweet-natured. Almond-shaped green eyes.

Coat is dense but very silky, like sealskin

Heart-shaped face

Large ears

◄ KORAT
This strong, medium-sized cat comes from Thailand, where its name means "good fortune". Its glossy, silver-blue coat is tipped with silver. Very large, bright green eyes.

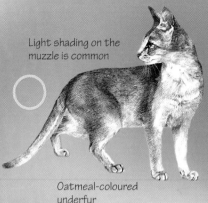

Light shading on the muzzle is common

Oatmeal-coloured underfur

◄ BLUE ABYSSINIAN

A muscular cat of Foreign type. Its underfur is pale cream or oatmeal, its top coat blue, ticked with a darker steel blue. An uncommon variety. Amber, hazel or green eyes.

➡ BLUE LONGHAIR

This cat's coat can be any shade of blue, preferably evenly-coloured all over. The kittens may be born with tabby markings; these eventually disappear. Copper or orange eyes.

Small, tufted ears, set well apart

Short legs

➡ BLUE BURMESE

Burmese cats have a heavier build than most Foreign cats, but all are elegant and have fine coats. This variety has a silver-grey coat. Its face, ears and feet have a pale silver sheen. Yellow eyes.

Back and tail are only slightly darker than the rest of the coat

17

LILAC CATS

Lilac cats were first produced by breeding together blue and chocolate-coloured cats. Their coats are a delicate dove-grey, with a pinkish tinge.

➡ FOREIGN LILAC
A graceful cat of Foreign type. First produced by breeding Havana and Lilac-point Siamese cats. Its coat is an even frosty grey, tinged with pink. Green eyes.

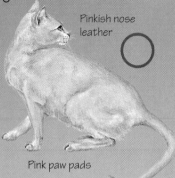

Pinkish nose leather

Pink paw pads

Tufted ears

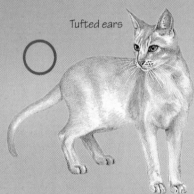

⬅ LILAC ABYSSINIAN
A very rare Foreign variety. Like all Abyssinian cats, this cat is strong, intelligent and graceful. The ideal coat colouring is pale pinkish grey, ticked with darker grey.

➡ LILAC BURMESE
Fairly thickset for a Foreign cat. Its coat is a pale lilac, often darker on its ears and mask. The kittens have shell-pink noses and paw pads, which later turn lavender pink. Golden-yellow eyes.

Ears are set wide apart

CREAM CATS

Cream cats' fur may be any shade of cream that does not have a "hot" (orange) tinge. Cream is a dilute form of red in cats.

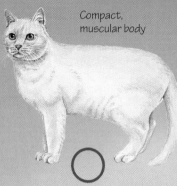

Compact, muscular body

← CREAM SHORTHAIR

This pale cream British Shorthair is hard to breed without tabby markings. Cream kittens born with stripes may lose their markings, but these can return later in life. Orange or copper eyes.

→ CREAM LONGHAIR

A Longhair cat with a pale to medium coat. Cream Longhairs are bred with White Longhairs to stop the cream colour from becoming too hot. Deep copper eyes.

There should be no markings on the coat

Dark shading on the ears

← CREAM BURMESE

A Foreign cat with a rich cream coat. The breed standard allows faint tabby markings on the face, but not on the sides or belly. Pink nose and paw pads. Golden-yellow eyes.

19

WHITE CATS

To meet the breed standard, a white cat should be pure white all over, with no traces of coloured markings. Some white cats may be deaf.

⬇ WHITE SHORTHAIR

This white cat has a typical British Shorthair build. It may have blue eyes, orange eyes or one blue eye and one orange eye. White cats with an eye of each colour are called Odd-eyed Whites.

Blue-eyed White

Odd-eyed White

Orange-eyed White

Large, pricked ears

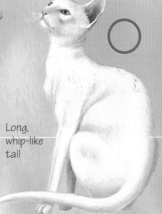
Long, whip-like tail

➡ FOREIGN WHITE

This cat is like a Siamese cat without dark points. It has a slim, elegant body and a smooth, sparkling white coat. Blue eyes are the only breed standard colour, but yellow and odd-eyed varieties do exist.

Blue-eyed White

◄ WHITE LONGHAIR

The best examples of this breed have a typical Longhair shape, but in some cats the body, nose and ears are longer than usual. It may have blue eyes, orange eyes or odd-coloured eyes (one blue, one orange).

Tufted ears

Full cheeks

Orange-eyed White

Odd-eyed White

➡ CHINCHILLA

An unusually dainty Longhair. Its chin, ear tufts, belly and chest are pure white. The rest of its coat is tipped with black, making the coat seem to sparkle. Emerald or blue-green eyes and brick red nose.

Eyes and tip of nose are outlined in black

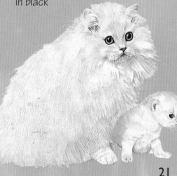

21

BROWN CATS

The colour of brown cats' fur ranges from a warm
chestnut to the colour of dark chocolate.

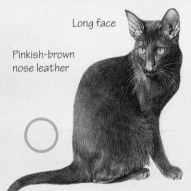

Long face

Pinkish-brown
nose leather

← HAVANA
So called because it is
the colour of a Havana
cigar. Rich brown coat,
without markings. Foreign
type. Green eyes.

➡ BROWN BURMESE
Seal brown coat,
without shading.
Golden eyes.

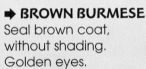

**← CHOCOLATE
BURMESE**
Milk chocolate coloured
coat with darker brown
points. Golden eyes.

There is often a
dark line down
the spine

**➡ NORMAL OR
RUDDY ABYSSINIAN**
Ruddy brown coat, ticked with
black or brown. Foreign type.
Amber, green or hazel eyes.

TABBY PATTERNED CATS

Tabby patterned cats (see also pages 8-9) have coats of two tones of the same colour, which appear in clear patterns of stripes or spots. White patches are forbidden in some show-standard breeds.

➡ RED MACKEREL TABBY SHORTHAIR
A British Shorthair with a rich orange-red coat and deep red Mackerel Tabby markings. Hazel, green or orange eyes.

Stripes from spine to belly

➡ RED CLASSIC TABBY SHORTHAIR
A British Shorthair with a rich orange-red coat with deeper Classic Tabby markings. Hazel, green or orange eyes.

M-mark

"Poached-egg-on-toast" mark

Small, tufted ears

⬅ RED TABBY LONGHAIR
A typical Longhair. Its coat is a rich orange-red with dark red markings. Classic Tabby markings are usual. Large copper eyes.

23

TABBY PATTERNED CATS

➡ BROWN CLASSIC TABBY SHORTHAIR

Sable brown or rich brown coat with black Classic Tabby markings. Orange, hazel or deep yellow eyes.

Vertical stripes

⬅ BROWN MACKEREL TABBY SHORTHAIR

Black Mackerel Tabby markings on a rich brown or sable brown coat. A rare British Shorthair. Orange, hazel or deep yellow eyes.

Spots run down length of spine

➡ BROWN SPOTTED SHORTHAIR

Has the sturdy build and short, close coat of a British Shorthair. Its coat is brown with lots of clear black spots. Orange, hazel or deep yellow eyes.

➡ RED SPOTTED SHORTHAIR

A British Shorthair bred from the Red Mackerel Tabby Shorthair. Its spots should be well-defined. Red coat with spots of a deeper red. Bright copper eyes.

Face has tabby markings

⬅ BROWN TABBY LONGHAIR

It is difficult to breed good examples of this Longhair cat, so it is quite rare. Its coat is a rich, coppery brown, with black Classic Tabby markings. Large, round hazel or copper eyes.

Large ears

Broken rings under the chin

➡ BRONZE ORIENTAL SPOTTED TABBY

This elegant, medium-sized Foreign cat was bred from Siamese cats. Its fine coat is bronze coloured, with rich chocolate brown spots. Green eyes with black rims.

25

TABBY PATTERNED CATS

➡ SILVER TABBY SHORTHAIR

This British Shorthair has a beautiful silver and black coat. Either Classic or Mackerel Tabby markings. Brick red or black nose leather. Green or hazel eyes.

Silver Mackerel Tabby Shorthair

Silver Classic Tabby Shorthair

Full, silvery ruff

⬅ SILVER TABBY LONGHAIR

This cat's pale silver coat has clearly-defined black markings. Classic Tabby pattern only. Green or hazel eyes.

➡ SILVER SPOTTED SHORTHAIR

A British Shorthair cat bred from Silver Mackerel Tabby Shorthairs. Its coat is silver with black spots. Tabby markings on its head. Green or hazel eyes.

Tail may have spots or broken rings

BI-COLOURED CATS

Bi-coloured cats have coats of two basic colours, one of which is usually white. The other colour may be plain or tabby patterned. Many breed standards state that not more than half of the cat's body should be white.

➡ RED AND WHITE BI-COLOUR LONGHAIR

In show-standard cats, not more than half of the coat may be white, and not more than two-thirds red. Longhair build. Round copper or orange eyes.

White blaze between eyes

Short, thick legs

Face has patches of colour

White blaze between eyes

⬅ RED AND WHITE BI-COLOUR SHORTHAIR

This cat's coat is patched in red and white in the same proportions as the Red and White Bi-colour Longhair. British Shorthair build. Orange, yellow or copper eyes.

BI-COLOURED CATS

➡ BLUE-CREAM LONGHAIR

The blue and cream shades in this cat's soft, silky coat merge together. The few males of this colour are sterile (cannot breed). Deep copper or orange eyes.

Light-coloured fur

➡ BLUE-CREAM SHORTHAIR

The blue and cream in this British Shorthair's coat merge softly. Breed standard forbids white or tabby patches. Almost always female. Copper, orange or yellow eyes.

Short, dense fur with colours merging softly together

Fur colours should merge together

⬅ BLUE-CREAM BURMESE

Its body is elegant, but quite thickset for a Foreign cat. As with other Blue-Cream breeds, these cats are almost always female. Golden yellow eyes.

➡ BLUE AND WHITE BI-COLOUR SHORTHAIR

This compact, muscular Shorthair is fairly rare. Its coat may be up to two-thirds blue and up to one-half white. Brilliant copper or orange eyes.

Short, thick coat

⬅ BLUE AND WHITE BI-COLOUR LONGHAIR

Not often seen. A Longhair with silky, flowing fur. Up to a half of its coat may be white, and up to two-thirds blue. Deep copper or orange eyes.

Thick, silky ruff and frill

➡ BLUE SMOKE AND WHITE LONGHAIR

This cat's underfur is ash-white, and its top coat blue, shading to silver on its sides. Its mask and feet are blue, and its frill and ear tufts silver. Orange or copper eyes.

Pale underfur shows clearly when cat moves

BI-COLOURED CATS

➡ CREAM SPOTTED AND WHITE SHORTHAIR

Tabby markings on face

A rare British Shorthair with a pale cream coat patterned in well-defined cream spots. It may have tabby markings on its head. Orange or copper eyes.

⬅ CREAM AND WHITE BI-COLOUR SHORTHAIR

To meet the breed standard, up to one half of this rare British Shorthair's coat should be white, and up to two-thirds cream. Bright copper or orange eyes.

➡ CREAM AND WHITE BI-COLOUR LONGHAIR

Face is patched with cream and white

This cat's coat is patterned like the Cream and White Bi-colour Shorthair. The breed standard does not allow tabby markings. Longhair build. Orange or copper eyes.

Back often has
a reddish tinge

Faint auburn
rings on tail

◄ TURKISH VAN CAT
A sturdy, long-bodied cat
from Turkey. Has a shorter
coat, longer face and
less chunky body than
most Longhairs. Chalk-
white coat with auburn
(reddish-brown) markings
on its face and tail.
Round amber eyes.

➡ BLACK AND WHITE
BI-COLOUR SHORTHAIR
A show-standard cat has a
coat up to two-thirds black
and one-half white, with
no stray white hairs in the
black. British Shorthair build.
Orange or copper eyes.

Full
tail

Small, tufted ears,
set well apart

➡ BLACK AND WHITE
BI-COLOUR LONGHAIR
A Longhair with the same
colourings as the Black
and White Bi-colour
Shorthair. Bi-colour cats
are often bigger than other
Longhairs. Copper eyes.

31

SMOKE COLOURED CATS

Smoke coloured cats can have a variety of base colours, such as blue, black or cream. Each hair is a lighter colour at the base than at the tip.

➡ BRITISH TIPPED SHORTHAIR

Similar in colouring to the Chinchilla (page 21). Its top coat and underfur are white, but the top coat is tipped with black. Broad, round head. Green eyes.

Eyes and tip of nose are outlined in black

⬅ SMOKE SHORTHAIR

This British Shorthair has a black top coat and silver underfur, which shows when it moves. Show-standard cats should have no stray white hairs among the black. Orange or yellow eyes.

Silvery ear tufts

⬅ BLACK SMOKE LONGHAIR

A longhaired cat with ash-white underfur. The top coat is also ash-white, with black tips. Its ruff, ear tufts and sides are silvery. Orange or copper eyes.

← SHELL CAMEO

Cameo cats, like Chinchillas (page 21), have white underfur with a tipped top coat. The white top coat is tipped with pale cream or red, giving the fur a rose-pink haze. Longhair build. Rich copper eyes with pink rims.

→ SHADED CAMEO

This is a darker form of the Shell Cameo. Its white top coat is lightly tipped with red, so that the coat looks a reddish-pink. Rich copper eyes with pink rims.

Red tipping gives coat a sparkling appearance

Dark mask

← SMOKE CAMEO

The darkest Cameo cat. At first glance, its coat looks all red, because the top coat is tipped with red, but the white underfur shows when it moves. Long, silky coat. Rich copper eyes with pink rims.

33

MULTI-COLOURED CATS

In order to meet their breed standard, most types of multi coloured cat must not have strong tabby markings. Most of the cats on these two pages are Tortoiseshell cats (often called Torties, for short). Male Tortoiseshell cats are very rare, and are almost always unable to breed.

➡ TORTOISESHELL SHORTHAIR
This British Shorthair has a black coat with red and cream patches. Almost always female. If a female Tortoiseshell is mated with a red male, all the female kittens will be tortoiseshell or red. Orange or copper eyes.

➡ TORTOISESHELL AND WHITE SHORTHAIR
A white cat with red, cream and black patches. Usually has more tortoiseshell areas than white, with coloured patches on the head, ears, tail, back and sides. British Shorthair build. Orange, hazel or copper eyes.

White blaze between eyes

➡ TORTOISESHELL LONGHAIR

This Longhair's coat has evenly distributed and broken-up patches of red, cream and black. Copper or deep orange eyes.

Extra-long frill

White blaze between eyes

⬅ TORTOISESHELL AND WHITE LONGHAIR

This cat's coat has separate patches of red, cream and black. It has some white on its face, chest, legs and feet. Always female. Deep orange or copper eyes.

Patches of colour are not clearly defined

➡ CHOCOLATE TORTIE BURMESE

This cat's coat is a mixture of various shades of chocolate and red. Other Tortie Burmese include the Brown/Normal Tortie Burmese, from which this cat was first bred. Foreign type. Yellow eyes.

35

MONGREL CATS

The cats on this page are known as mongrels. This means that their parents are of mixed breeds. Mongrel tabby cats, which you are very likely to see in your neighbourhood, often have white patches.

➡ RED TABBY AND WHITE
This cat is classed as a mongrel because pure-bred Red Tabbies should not have white fur, and pure-bred two-coloured cats should not have strong tabby markings.

Mongrel tabbies often have a white chest and paws

⬅ SILVER TABBY AND WHITE
This pretty shorthaired cat could not enter a class for Silver Tabbies at a cat show because of its white patches, although it may win a non-pedigree class.

➡ BROWN TABBY AND WHITE
Since it has a white ruff as well as tabby stripes, this longhaired cat does not fit any breed standard. Tabby markings are common in litters of mongrel kittens.

POINTED CATS

Pointed cats have white, off-white or cream coats with points (legs, paws, ears, tail and face) of a contrasting colour. Kittens are white all over when born and the points take several months to develop fully.

➡ SEAL-POINT SIAMESE
This cat's cream coat shades to fawn on its back. It has seal-brown (dark brown) points. Siamese cats' coats tend to darken with age. Foreign type. Deep blue eyes.

This four-week old kitten has just started to develop its points

Kittens are white all over at birth

Whip-like tail

➡ CHOCOLATE-POINT SIAMESE
This cat has an ivory coat with milk chocolate coloured points. Foreign type. Sapphire blue eyes.

➡ BLUE-POINT SIAMESE
An attractive cat with pale blue points and a white coat, shading to light blue on its back. Foreign type. Sapphire blue eyes.

Very fine, close-textured coat

POINTED CATS

Fine, coloured lines called "tracings" run from the ears to the mask

← RED-POINT SIAMESE
Originally bred from Seal-point Siamese cats and Red Tabby Shorthairs. Its clear white coat shades to apricot on its back. Reddish-gold points. Foreign type. Bright blue eyes.

➡ LILAC-POINT SIAMESE
This cat has an off-white coat, shading to a pale pinkish-grey on its back. The points are also pinkish-grey. Foreign type. Blue eyes, sometimes paler than those of other Siamese cats.

Coat does not usually darken with age

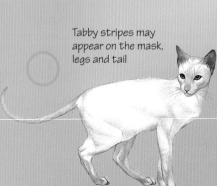

Tabby stripes may appear on the mask, legs and tail

← CREAM-POINT SIAMESE
A white cat with some tabby markings. Its face and legs are the colour of clotted cream, and its nose, ears and tail are a warm apricot. Foreign type. Bright blue eyes.

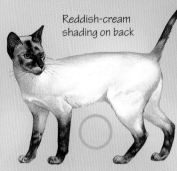

Reddish-cream shading on back

← TORTIE-POINT SIAMESE

This cat is always female. Its points have patches of red and/or cream, with either blue, lilac, seal or chocolate. The rest of the coat is cream or fawn. Foreign type. Blue eyes.

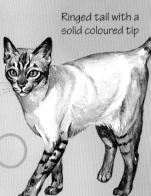

Ringed tail with a solid coloured tip

➡ TABBY-POINT SIAMESE

This cat has a pale coat with tabby markings instead of coloured points. The markings appear in any of the usual Siamese colours. Foreign type. Blue eyes.

➡ SEAL COLOURPOINT OR SEAL-POINT HIMALAYAN

Colourpoints (called Himalayans in the USA) are Longhairs with Siamese-type colouring. This one has a cream coat and seal brown points. Breed standard forbids Foreign-type features. Bright blue eyes.

Broad, round head

Low, sturdy body

39

POINTED CATS

← CHOCOLATE COLOURPOINT OR CHOCOLATE-POINT HIMALAYAN
This Longhair's Siamese-type points are a warm milk chocolate colour. The rest of the coat is ivory. Clear, bright blue eyes.

Long, thick, soft coat

➡ LILAC COLOURPOINT OR LILAC-POINT HIMALAYAN
This magnolia-coloured cat has frosty grey points, tinged with pink. Its nose and paw pads are lavender pink. Longhair type. Clear, bright blue eyes.

Small, tufted ears, set well apart

➡ BLUE COLOURPOINT OR BLUE-POINT HIMALAYAN
This Longhair cat has a cold, bluish-white coat with a pure white chest and stomach. Its points are blue. The coat may darken with age. Clear, bright blue eyes.

Short, full tail

Ear tufts

Round cheeks

← TORTIE COLOURPOINT OR TORTIE-POINT HIMALAYAN
The coat is cream with seal, red and/or cream points. This variety is always female. Longhair type. Blue eyes.

➡ RED COLOURPOINT OR FLAME-POINT HIMALAYAN
Gentle and affectionate, like all Colourpoints. Its coat is a creamy white with sandy orange points. Longhair type. Bright blue eyes.

← CREAM COLOURPOINT OR CREAM-POINT HIMALAYAN
This variety of Colourpoint has a white coat with rich cream to apricot points. Longhair type. Blue eyes.

POINTED CATS

→ SEAL-POINT BIRMAN
Birmans are stocky, long-bodied cats with round, wide heads. Their fur is long and silky. This type has a creamy coat with seal brown points. Blue eyes.

→ BLUE-POINT BIRMAN
Just like the Seal-point Birman, but its points are blue-grey. Birman kittens develop their points after several weeks. Grey nose. Blue eyes.

Long, bushy tail

White "gloves"

Large, pointed ears

← SEAL-POINT BALINESE
This medium-sized, graceful cat is really a longhaired Siamese cat, not a Longhair. It has a pale coat with seal brown, Siamese-type points. Balinese cats are also bred in other Siamese colours. Blue eyes.

Long, full tail

UNUSUAL CATS

The cats on pages 43 to 47 belong to unusual or recently-developed breeds. Many of these are rare outside the country where they first appeared.

➡ CORNISH REX
"Rex" is the name given to this cat's waved fur. Even its whiskers and eyebrows are curly. The breed first appeared by chance in an ordinary Shorthair litter in Cornwall, England. Any colour.

Arched back

Long, thin, whip-like tail

Crinkled whiskers

⬅ DEVON REX
This dainty cat first appeared in a litter of farm kittens in Devon, England. Its softly-waved coat is thinner than that of the Cornish Rex. Large, wide-set eyes. Any colour.

Wedge-shaped head

➡ CHOCOLATE-POINT SI-REX
The Si-Rex is a cross between a Devon Rex and a Siamese cat. Si-Rex cats have pale, curly coats with Siamese points. Blue eyes.

UNUSUAL CATS

Broad, round rump

← MANX CAT
Manx Cats are named after the Isle of Man, one of the first places where they appeared. This variety has long back legs and a short back, with no trace of a tail. Thick underfur and soft top coat. Any colour.

Longish nose

Manx cats' litters may include kittens with tails, kittens with small "stumpy" tails, or tailless "rumpy" kittens

Rumpy kitten

"Stump"

Chubby cheeks

→ STUMPY MANX
This variety of Manx Cat has a very short tail. It is less likely to suffer from the spine and bowel problems associated with rumpy Manx Cats. Otherwise identical to tailless variety. Any colour.

Round rump, with
no sign of a tail

← CYMRIC
This breed of cat is
identical to the tailless
Manx Cat, except
that it has a long
coat. May be any
colour or pattern.

Usually crouches, so its
long back legs look shorter
than they actually are

→ JAPANESE BOBTAIL
An ancient breed from
Japan with a muscular,
narrow body. Its soft coat
is traditionally red, black
and white. Its tail is very
short, carried curled up. It
has slanting eyes, strong
cheekbones and very
long back legs.

The folded ears are hard
to clean properly, so
infections are common

→ SCOTTISH FOLD
This breed developed
by chance from an
ordinary Scottish litter.
The kittens are born with
pricked ears which droop
as they become older.
Many breeders disapprove
of breeding cats with such
deformities. British Shorthair
type. Any colour.

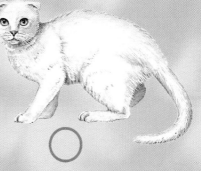

45

UNUSUAL CATS

➡ MAINE COON
So-called because its fur looks like a raccoon's coat. Heavily built, with a shaggy coat. It has long hair on its belly and back legs, but quite a short ruff. Green, gold, blue or copper eyes.

Longish face

Similar in shape to the Turkish Van cat, but more muscular

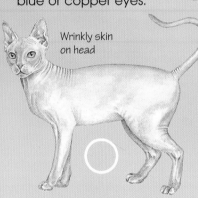

Wrinkly skin on head

Ears, paws and tail-tip have the most noticable down

⬅ SPHYNX
This odd-looking cat has practically no fur on its body. It has short, velvety fur on its face and back and light, downy fur on its legs and paws. Skin may be patterned with dark patches. Any colour. Golden eyes.

➡ AMERICAN WIREHAIR
A lively, inquisitive cat bred from a wiry-haired cat born in an ordinary litter. The fur on its head, sides and tail is harsh and crinkled. The fur on its underparts is softer. Any colour.

Crinkly whiskers and eyebrows

Tufted ears with dark tips

A dark line runs down the spine to the tip of the tail

➡ SOMALI

A longhaired version of the Abyssinian cat. Its coat can be orangey-brown with black ticking, or a warm red with chocolate brown ticking. Alert and lively. Gold or green eyes.

Short, blunt-ended tail

➡ EXOTIC SHORTHAIR

This breed was developed in the USA from shorthaired and longhaired cats. Medium-length fur, a short, body and a broad head. Any Longhair colour or pattern.

Coat shines like patent leather

Short, thick legs

⬅ BOMBAY

This muscular, medium-sized cat was bred from Burmese cats and shorthaired cats. Its black coat is short, fine and very shiny. Gold or deep copper eyes.

47

CAT BEHAVIOUR

When you go out spotting cats, you can also watch how they behave. Pages 48 to 54 show some of the things you can look out for.

➡ JUMPING DOWN
Cats can jump down from quite high places without damage. Their flexible skeleton and cushioned paw pads absorb the shock of landing. The position of tail, head and legs is very important for balance.

Legs outstretched for landing

⬅ JUMPING UP
For their size, cats can jump much higher and further than people. With their strong hind legs, and hind paws that give them a firm push off, they can spring up from a sitting position.

Sharp claws help cats to climb

➡ CLIMBING
Cats are excellent climbers. Their claws and the rough surface of their paw pads give them a good grip.

➡ SENSE OF TOUCH

A cat's paw pads are very sensitive to touch and pressure. Cats use their paws to investigate strange objects and to touch prey to see if it is dead.

Cats sometimes mark out their territory by scratching trees

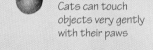

Cats can touch objects very gently with their paws

⬅ SHARPENING CLAWS

Cats have sharp claws for killing prey and for climbing. The claws stay sharp because the outer layer comes off with wear. Cats often scratch against trees or other hard surfaces to help remove this outer layer.

➡ EATING GRASS

Cats often eat grass, which helps their digestion. Also, cats swallow fur when they wash, which collects in balls inside their stomach. Eating grass helps them to vomit up these fur balls.

49

SLEEPING AND STRETCHING

➡ SLEEPING

Cats spend a lot of time sleeping very lightly. This is called "catnapping", and the cat can wake from it instantly. Cats sleep deeply when they feel secure.

⬅ ARCHING BACK

Upon waking from a deep sleep, cats go through a routine of stretching movements to loosen their joints and prepare them for action. First, the back is arched up like this.

➡ STRETCHING FRONT LEGS

Next, the cat stretches out its front legs as far as they will go, forcing its bottom up in the air.

⬅ STRETCHING BACK LEGS

Finally, each back leg is raised in turn and stretched out behind as far as it will go.

WASHING

← WASHING SIDE OF THE BODY

To wash and groom the side of its body, a cat stretches itself out like this. It uses its teeth to tease out any burrs or knots in the fur.

This washing position is sometimes called the "Yoga position"

← WASHING HINDQUARTERS

A cat can bend almost double to wash its hindquarters and the base of its tail. It twists its body to balance with one leg in the air. Its rough tongue is used to comb as well as wash its fur.

➡ WASHING FACE AND EARS

Cats wash their face and ears with their front paws. The paw is licked to make it damp, then wiped round the ear, over the head and down over the eye. This is repeated several times, with each paw washing one side of the head.

The right paw is used to wash the right side of the head, and vice versa

51

HUNTING

A cat creeps forward, watching its prey intently

← STALKING
Cats can keep still for hours, watching quietly for prey. When a cat spots a possible victim, it begins to stalk. It crouches low, with its head, body and tail almost level, and moves silently forward.

Preparing for the final spring

→ FREEZING
When a cat gets close to its prey, it freezes low and prepares itself for the final dash and spring. Its bottom is raised and the tip of its tail twitches in excitement.

← POUNCING
Finally, the cat lunges forward, pinning the prey down with its forepaws. Often the "prey" is just a leaf or some other small object, but if it is an animal, the cat may kill it with a bite to the neck.

SMELLING

➡ FLEHMEN REACTION
Sense of smell is very important to cats. As well as smelling through their nose, they open their mouths and draw air into channels in the roof of their mouth which connect to a special scent organ. This is called the Flehmen reaction.

The lips are drawn back like this in the Flehmen reaction

⬅ SHOWING FRIENDSHIP
Cats use scent to show friendship and ownership. They mark people and objects with scent from glands on their head and tail, by rubbing up against them. People cannot smell this scent.

➡ MARKING TERRITORY
Male cats mark their home area or territory out by backing up to objects and spraying them with strong-smelling urine. The scent tells other cats "This is my territory".

If a male cat is neutered when a few months old, it will be less likely to spray

FRIENDS AND FOES

➡ FRIENDSHIP
Friendly cats greet
each other by
touching noses and
whiskers, and sniffing
the forehead, lips and
chin, where there are
scent glands.

The cat may also
hiss and spit

⬅ AGGRESSION
A cat may adopt this
aggressive pose if it feels
threatened by another
animal. The back is arched,
the tail is held up stiffly and
the fur stands on end. This
makes the cat look larger and
helps to warn off enemies.

Ears are
held back

➡ FEAR
A frightened cat will back
off as far as possible if it is
cornered by an enemy.
Its eyes may dart
nervously about and it
may raise a paw, ready
to strike out if the enemy
comes too close.

LOOKING AFTER YOUR CAT

All kittens should have injections at about 12 weeks old to protect them from disease. Your cat should also be neutered at about six months old. This is a simple operation which prevents a cat from having kittens.

Cats sometimes have parasites. These are small animals, such as fleas and tapeworms, which live on or in an animal's body. You can get rid of parasites using medicine from a vet. If a cat has fleas, it will scratch a lot. Cat fleas can bite humans, but they don't live on them.

PLAYTIME
Most cats are naturally playful. Try dragging some string along the floor, or giving your cat a ball with a bell inside to chase. All cats are hunters, so you may see your pet pounce like a jungle cat.

SHARPENING CLAWS
Cats also scratch, to keep their claws sharp. If you train your cat to use a scratching post like the one below, it won't scratch the furniture. If you see your cat scratching around the house, pick it up and take it to the scratching post.

This scratching post has rough rope wound around it. Others may be wrapped in carpet.

CHOOSING A PET KITTEN

Think carefully before you buy a pet cat. It will need care and attention for all of its life, and you will have to pay for food and medical treatment. It's best to buy a kitten rather than an adult cat, as they adapt to a new home and family more easily.

Animal shelters or private breeders are good places to get a kitten. If you can, try to see the parents. If they seem healthy and well-cared for, the kitten probably will be too. Never buy a kitten that looks dirty or ill.

Look for these features:

Bright eyes

Clean ears

Clean nose

Full set of teeth

Healthy coat

Sturdy limbs

Clean and dry under tail

PREPARATION

Kittens are ready to leave their mother at 8-12 weeks old. Before you bring your kitten home, you will need the items listed below.

- A litter tray and cat litter. Your cat will need these for going to the toilet indoors.

- Food (check that the label on the packet or can says "complete")

- Cat toys

- Food and water bowls. Make sure they have fairly shallow sides.

- A cat brush. A cat's coat must be brushed regularly to prevent knots, especially in longhaired cats.

- A cat basket. You can make one from a large cardboard box with a section cut out of one side. Line it with newspaper and put a soft blanket inside.

SETTLING DOWN

You can help your kitten feel more comfortable when it arrives by wrapping a hot water bottle in a towel and putting it in the kitten's basket. This feels like a mother cat's warm body.

Even a cardboard box can make a cosy cat basket. Blankets and newspapers will keep warmth inside the box.

At first, your kitten will nervously explore its new home. Crouch down and hold out your hand so that your kitten can smell it. Talk quietly to your kitten to keep it calm. When your kitten is relaxed, it may start to wash itself.

Kittens learn about new things by sniffing them. A pet cat quickly learns its new owner's smell.

USEFUL WORDS

bi-colour - cat with a coat that is white and one other colour. The coat of a show-standard cat should be no more than one-half white.

blaze - a line of colour in the middle of a cat's face.

breed standard - the ideal characteristics of a cat breed, as agreed by breeders. Few cats have every characteristic.

breeding true - producing kittens that look very similar to their parents.

fur balls - fur swallowed during washing that collects in a mass in the cat's stomach.

litter - one or more kittens born at the same time.

mask - a cat's face.

mongrel - a cat of mixed or unknown parentage. Also known as a mixed-breed.

nose leather - the skin on the end of a cat's nose.

paw pads - soft pads of skin on the bottom of a cat's paws.

pedigree - a recognized breed of cat whose ancestors have been registered with a national organization, such as the GCCF, for at least three generations.

persian - another name for a longhaired cat.

points - markings on a cat's face, legs, tail and ears.

pure-breed - a cat whose ancestors have been of the same breed for at least four generations.

queen - an un-neutered female cat.

self - cat of a single overall colour.

ticking - having hairs which are broken up by bands of colour. Only found in Abyssinian cats.

tipping - having fur of one colour with darker tips.

tom - an un-neutered male cat.

tortie - another name for a tortoiseshell cat.

whiskers - the pressure-sensitive hairs on a cat's face.

whisker pads - muscular pads above the mouth from which the whiskers grow.

WEß SITES

If you have access to the Internet, you can find out more about cats online. Here are some Web sites to visit:

The Governing Council of the Cat Fancy (GCCF) – Official Web site of the UK's leading cat organization. **ourworld.compuserve.com/ homepages/GCCF_CATS/ welcome.htm**

Fédération Internationale Féline (FIFe) – A major European cat organization. **www.fife.org**

The New South Wales Cat Fanciers' Association – A large cat organization based in Australia. **www.hotkey.net.au/~nswcfa**

Worldwide cat clubs – A list of all-breed cat clubs and organizations around the world, with Web links. **www.netpets.org/cats/ catclub/allbreed.html**

Cat Breeds – A searchable database of cat breeds, with images and thorough descriptions. **www.felinebreeds.com**

The Cat Fanciers' Association (CFA) – A registry of pedigree cats. Includes information about cat shows and breeds. **www.cfainc.org**

Cat Fanciers – Lots of useful information, including frequently asked questions and many Web links. **www.fanciers.com**

Supreme Cat Show – The GCCF's official UK show. **www.chace.demon.co.uk/**

Pedigree cats – Information on pedigree cats in the UK. **www.palantir.co.uk/gccf.html**

Cats Protection – The UK's largest cat charity. Use this Web site to find the location of your nearest rescue shelter. **cats.org.uk**

RSPCA (Royal Society for the Prevention of Cruelty to Animals) – An animal care and rescue charity in the UK. **www.rspca.org**

PDSA (People's Dispensary for Sick Animals) – A UK charity which cares for injured and sick animals. **pdsa.org.uk**

CHECKLIST

The cats and behaviours in this checklist have been arranged in alphabetical order. Every time you spot a new breed or a new type of behaviour, you can fill in the date on which you saw it. You may also want to keep your own record of where you saw it, e.g. on the street or at a show.

Name of breed	Date spotted	Name of breed	Date spotted
Abyssinian, Blue		Blue Longhair	
Abyssinian, Lilac		Blue-Cream Longhair	
Abyssinian, Normal or Ruddy		Blue-Cream Shorthair	
Abyssinian, Red or Sorrel		Bombay	
American Wire Hair		British Blue	
Balinese (any colour)		British Tipped Shorthair	
Bi-colour Longhair, Black and White		Brown Tabby and White (longhaired)	
Bi-colour Longhair, Blue and White		Brown Tabby and White (shorthaired)	
Bi-colour Longhair, Cream and White		Burmese, Blue	
Bi-colour Longhair, Red and White		Burmese, Blue-Cream	
Bi-colour Shorthair, Black and White		Burmese, Brown	
Bi-colour Shorthair, Blue and White		Burmese, Chocolate	
Bi-colour Shorthair, Cream and White		Burmese, Chocolate Tortie	
Bi-colour Shorthair, Red and White		Burmese, Cream	
Birman, Blue-point		Burmese, Lilac	
Birman, Seal-point		Burmese, Red	
Black Longhair		Cameo, Shaded	
Black Shorthair		Cameo, Shell	

Name of breed	Date spotted	Name of breed	Date spotted
Cameo, Smoke		Red Tabby and White (longhaired)	
Chinchilla		Red Tabby and White (shorthaired)	
Colourpoint, Blue		Rex, Cornish	
Colourpoint, Chocolate		Rex, Devon	
Colourpoint, Cream		Russian Blue	
Colourpoint, Lilac		Scottish Fold	
Colourpoint, Red		Siamese, Blue-point	
Colourpoint, Seal		Siamese, Chocolate-point	
Colourpoint, Tortie		Siamese, Cream-point	
Cream Longhair		Siamese, Lilac-point	
Cream Shorthair		Siamese, Red-point	
Cymric		Siamese, Seal-point	
Exotic Shorthair		Siamese, Tabby-point	
Foreign Black		Siamese, Tortie-point	
Foreign Lilac		Silver Tabby and White (longhaired)	
Foreign White		Silver Tabby and White (shorthaired)	
Havana		Si-Rex (any colour)	
Japanese Bobtail		Smoke Longhair, Black	
Korat		Smoke Longhair, Blue	
Maine Coon		Smoke Shorthair	
Manx, Rumpy		Somali	
Manx, Stumpy		Sphynx	
Oriental Spotted Tabby (any colour)		Spotted Shorthair, Brown	
Red Self Longhair		Spotted Shorthair, Cream	

Name of breed	Date spotted	Cat Behaviour	Date spotted
Spotted Shorthair, Red		Aggression	
Spotted Shorthair, Silver		Climbing	
Tabby Longhair, Brown		Eating Grass	
Tabby Longhair, Red		Fear	
Tabby Longhair, Silver		Flehmen reaction	
Tabby Shorthair, Brown Classic		Friendship (to other cats)	
Tabby Shorthair, Brown Mackerel		Friendship (to people)	
Tabby Shorthair, Red Classic		Hunting (stalking)	
Tabby Shorthair, Red Mackerel		Hunting (freezing)	
Tabby Shorthair, Silver Classic		Hunting (pouncing)	
Tabby Shorthair, Silver Mackerel		Jumping down	
Tortoiseshell Longhair		Jumping up	
Tortoiseshell Shorthair		Marking territory	
Tortoiseshell and White Longhair		Sharpening claws	
Tortoiseshell and White Shorthair		Sleeping	
Turkish Van		Stretching, arching back	
White Longhair, Blue-eyed		Stretching, back legs	
White Longhair, Odd- eyed		Stretching, front legs	
White Longhair, Orange-eyed		Touch (sense of)	
White Shorthair, Blue-eyed		Washing, face and ears	
White Shorthair, Odd-eyed		Washing, hindquarters	
White Shorthair, Orange-eyed		Washing, side of body	

INDEX